WHAT ARE PRODUCERS AND CONSUMERS?

MARCIA AMIDON LUSTED

Britannica®
Educational Publishing

IN ASSOCIATION WITH

ROSEN
EDUCATIONAL SERVICES

Published in 2017 by Britannica Educational Publishing (a trademark of Encyclopædia Britannica, Inc.) in association with The Rosen Publishing Group, Inc.

29 East 21st Street, New York, NY 10010

Distributed exclusively by Rosen Publishing.

To see additional Britannica Educational Publishing titles, go to rosenpublishing.com.

First Edition

Britannica Educational Publishing
J.E. Luebering: Executive Director, Core Editorial
Mary Rose McCudden: Editor, Britannica Student Encyclopedia

Rosen Publishing
Heather Moore Niver: Editor
Nelson Sá: Art Director
Brian Garvey: Designer
Cindy Reiman: Photography Manager
Heather Moore Niver: Photo Researcher

Library of Congress Cataloging-in-Publication Data

Names: Lèusted, Marcia Amidon, author.
Title: What are producers and consumers? / Marcia Amidon Lusted.
Description: First Edition. | New York : Britannica Educational Publishing,
  2017. | Series: Let's find out! Community economics | Includes bibliographical references and index.
Identifiers: ISBN 9781680484038 (library bound)
  | ISBN 9781680484113 (pbk.) | ISBN 9781680483796 (6-pack)
Subjects: LCSH: Businesspeople—Juvenile literature. |
  Industrialists—Juvenile literature. | Consumers—Juvenile literature.
Classification: LCC HB615 .L8777 2017 | DDC 338--dc23
LC record available at http://lccn.loc.gov/2016000998

Manufactured in the United States of America

CONTENTS

I MAKE IT, YOU WANT IT

Apple is one of the best-known brand names in computers and electronics. Apple is a producer. The company makes products, like iPads and iPhones. Consumers buy these products. Consumers continue to buy Apple products because

A **producer** is a person or company that provides goods or services. A **consumer** is someone who buys goods and services for their personal use. The word comes from "consume," which means "to use or to spend something."

Apple's iPhone is one of its best-known products.

they like how easy their devices are to use as well as the applications that work only on them. Apple users are loyal to the company and its products. They believe Apple makes superior products and will continue to

Apple's customers are known for being loyal to the company and its products.

buy them, even if they are expensive.

Apple and its customers are a good example of the relationship between producers and consumers. Apple attracts consumers and then holds on to them. They keep producing new products that consumers want. Because those products are often new and exciting, other people become Apple customers, too. Producers and consumers need each other. Producers make money, and consumers get the things they want or need.

Buying and Selling

A society or a community creates wealth through buying and selling. Manufacturers make goods, or products. Sellers sell them to consumers. The money consumers pay keeps the producers in business. Consumers want more and more products and services. This means that producers make more things. More money is spent on goods and services than on anything else.

This economic cycle creates jobs for people

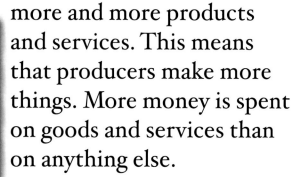

Consumers want more and more things to buy, keeping producers in business.

THINK ABOUT IT

Some people think that what consumers need and want shapes all of a society's economic activity. Do you think that is true? Why or why not?

in the community. They might make the products or sell the products that other people make. People with jobs have money to spend

The money that a community makes from taxes is used to pay for services such as a police force.

on goods and services. The sale of goods and services also brings money into the community through taxes. Taxes are fees that people pay to a government. They allow a community to pay for services like police and firefighters.

A Trip to the Store

Producers provide goods and consumers buy the goods. But what exactly are goods? They are things that are used or consumed, like food or clothing. Goods are also things that can be touched. Some are manufactured, such as computers and cars. Others are grown, such as fruits and vegetables. Consumers buy goods because they think

Almost everything for sale in a grocery store, such as these packages of cookies, is a type of good.

THINK ABOUT IT

Goods are something you can touch, and a service is something that someone does for you. Can you think of examples of goods and services that might be related?

Today, people can buy many of the goods they want online, using the Internet.

they will use them, either once or over and over again.

Almost everything that is for sale in a store is some kind of good. Goods can be a package of snacks at the grocery store, a new sweater from a department store, or a computer. Goods are also sold by mail and through the Internet.

LET ME DO THAT FOR YOU

A service is something that someone does for other people. It might be giving people haircuts or cleaning their houses. Firemen and police officers perform a service by putting out fires and enforcing laws. A service does not give the receivers something material. It provides something that they need and might not be able to do for

People who clean homes and offices are providing a service.

Not all services are provided for money. Volunteers provide services, like reading to children, without expecting payment.

themselves.

Some people who provide services are paid for their time but some are not. When people volunteer to read to older people at a nursing home or to help kids in a classroom, they are providing a service. The volunteers are not getting money for doing these activities, but they still provide a valuable service.

> A **volunteer** is someone who performs an activity or service for free.

FROM THE LAND

People who manufacture or produce goods need economic resources. These are things that can be used to make products or provide services. There are three kinds of economic resources. They are land, labor, and capital.

As an economic resource, land can mean a huge farm, a manufacturing

Labor resources include the workers in factories.

plant, or a tiny workshop. Land also includes natural resources. Some of these natural resources are renewable, like trees, animals, and crops. Others are nonrenewable, like oil and coal. It is important not to use up natural resources for producing goods.

Renewable resources are things that can be made or replaced easily. **Nonrenewable** resources are things that cannot be replaced. It takes millions of years for oil and coal to form, so they are nonrenewable.

A cow is an example of a renewable natural resource.

WORKERS WORKING

A blacksmith takes metal and makes goods like horseshoes and hardware.

Another kind of economic resource is labor, meaning the people who work for pay. Workers are needed to make materials into consumer goods. These materials might be natural resources or raw materials. Workers can produce goods

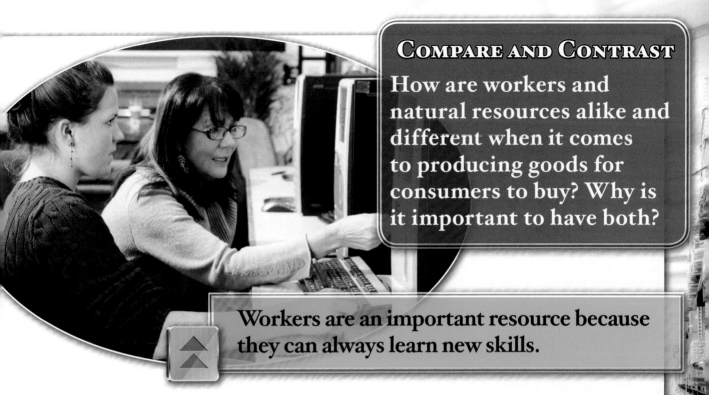

COMPARE AND CONTRAST
How are workers and natural resources alike and different when it comes to producing goods for consumers to buy? Why is it important to have both?

Workers are an important resource because they can always learn new skills.

or perform services.

Workers are a good economic resource because they can be used in different parts of the economy where they are needed. They can also learn to do new things. Unlike resources from nature, they can change depending on where they are needed. But they do need to be healthy and able to work.

Show Me the Money

The third type of economic resource is known as capital. Capital can be the actual money that companies use to produce goods or provide services. Companies use money to buy the materials they need to create goods or to build their service-based company. They might use money to buy buildings for manufacturing. Companies also use money to pay their workers.

A bakery must buy flour in order to make and sell bread.

Capital also includes the things that a company or business owns and uses to produce goods and services. This could be buildings, factories, equipment, vehicles, and machinery. Companies often buy these assets from other people or businesses. They might also build the assets themselves or pay to have someone build the assets for them. Others choose to rent them from someone else.

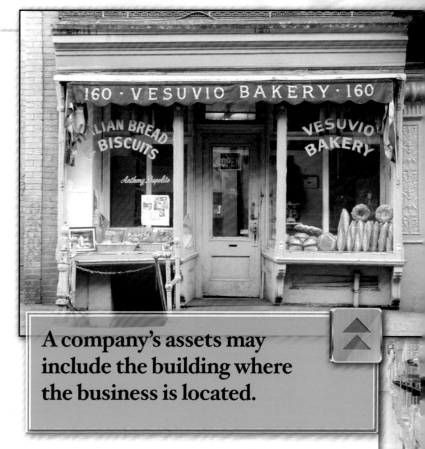

A company's assets may include the building where the business is located.

An **asset** is something that is useful or valuable. It may be property owned by a company or a person. An asset can be used to pay debts or to get loans.

WHO DOES WHAT?

Many companies manufacture or produce goods for consumers to buy. These companies are grouped together into industries. There are different categories of industries. Together these types of industries make a chain of production that brings finished goods or services to buyers.

Primary industries get the raw materials needed for making goods. They mine the Earth for metals or coal, operate drills to get oil from

Oil companies use pumps to extract oil from wells deep underground.

18

A furniture manufacturer needs raw materials like wood to make its products.

deep underground, or grow crops. Secondary industries take these raw materials and make them into something else. Oil can be turned into plastic products. Workers use steel and wood to make things like bridges, buildings, and furniture.

COMPARE AND CONTRAST

Think of several different examples of primary industries. Then think of several examples of secondary industries. Why do they need each other? How are they independent of one another?

More Industries

Creating goods and services for consumers takes even more types of industries. Tertiary industries refer to the companies that make it possible to make and sell products and services. Transportation and warehouse services help move the goods to the places where they can be sold. Advertising is designed to make consumers want the goods that are for sale. Tertiary industries also include services such as

Trucks carry goods from factories to stores. Trucking is therefore a tertiary industry.

Terms like primary (first), secondary (second), **tertiary** (third), **quaternary** (fourth), and quinary (fifth) are words for numbering things according to how important they are.

insurance, health care, and education.

Quaternary industries are businesses that have to do with technology and information. Workers in these industries include computer programmers, researchers in scientific labs, and people who develop new products. Some economists also include the quinary sector. This is the level of top executives and government officials.

Quaternary industries include research labs, which provide information and technology.

Buy, Buy, Buy

Manufacturers and producers create goods and services. But how do they get consumers to buy or use them? They use marketing and advertising (ads) to convince consumers that they need what those companies are selling. Marketing includes deciding which consumers are most likely to want a product or service. To sell a new toy,

Times Square in New York City is known for all the advertising signs found there.

THINK ABOUT IT

Tie-ins are a large part of advertising. Tie-ins are products—such as clothes, toys, and books—that are connected to a new movie. They are meant to build excitement about the movie.

Advertising tie-ins are used to create excitement about new movies.

a marketer will target kids. Parents are usually the ones who buy toys, so the marketer has to target them, too.

Marketing includes advertising. After a marketer decides which consumers are most likely to buy something, they create advertising for those groups. Ads can appear in many different places. They can be on television, on the Internet, in magazines or newspapers, and on billboards in public places.

SPEND, SPEND, SPEND

Where do people buy the goods and services after they see marketing and advertising? Today, there are many ways to shop. "Brick and mortar" stores are the traditional stores where people go to look at things before buying them. These stores can stand alone or be inside a shopping mall. If consumers are looking for a

COMPARE AND CONTRAST

What are the advantages of shopping online instead of visiting an actual store? What are the disadvantages of shopping online?

Shopping malls are still popular places for people to shop for goods.

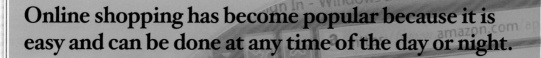

Online shopping has become popular because it is easy and can be done at any time of the day or night.

service, like carpet cleaning or window repair, they may call the company and have someone come to their home.

Today, many people shop online. They visit websites where they can choose what to buy and have it sent directly to their houses. Some people receive printed catalogs in the mail and then order what they want from the catalog's website. Others order from catalogs by sending an order form and a check through the mail.

A Consumer's Friend

Unfortunately, not every company that makes or sells goods, or provides services, is honest. Sometimes consumers end up with defective products. Companies often recall products that are defective. This means that consumers return the

If a product is **defective**, that means something is wrong with it and it does not perform the way it is supposed to. It may even be dangerous.

Some products are considered dangerous because they have a high level of lead in their paint.

Chair

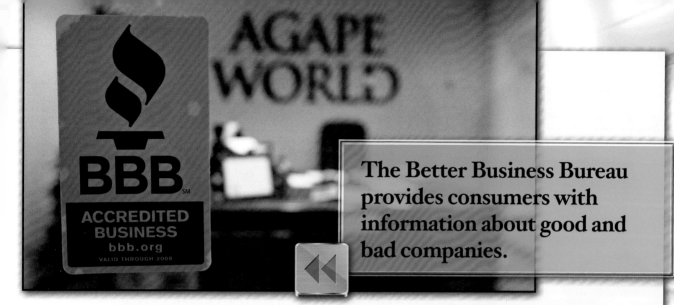

The Better Business Bureau provides consumers with information about good and bad companies.

products to the company and get their money back or have those products fixed or replaced. Sometimes a service does not do what it promised.

Consumers can research a company before they buy its goods or services. Magazines like *Consumer Reports* rate products. Organizations like the Better Business Bureau have records of good and bad companies. There are also websites that review products and services and let consumers know what is good and bad about them. Consumers need to protect themselves by doing research on companies and products before they spend their money.

It's All About Balance

A healthy economy needs the right balance of both producers and consumers. With too many producers and too few consumers, businesses that produce goods and services cannot sell enough to make money. With too many consumers and too few producers, people cannot buy enough of the goods and services they need.

The balance of producers and consumers also keeps a community healthy. Producers pay workers to

Just like a scale, a healthy economy needs to balance producers and consumers.

Buyers and sellers work together to build a healthy community.

make goods or carry out services. Those people, in turn, have money to be consumers themselves. This economic cycle balances sellers and buyers. It also helps a community provide jobs for the people who live there. The jobs generate taxes to keep the community running.

Taxes are money individuals and businesses pay to a government. Governments use the taxes to pay for services like road building, education, and fire protection.

GLOSSARY

advertising To call public attention to a product or service, especially by paid announcements.

catalog A list of goods for sale, along with their descriptions and prices.

crop A plant or animal, or a product from them, that can be grown and harvested.

cycle A series of events or actions that repeat themselves regularly and in the same order.

device A piece of equipment that serves a special purpose.

economic Relating to, or based on the production, distribution, and consumption of goods and services.

executive A person who manages or directs.

industry The businesses that provide a particular type of product or service.

insurance A contract by which someone guarantees for a fee to pay someone else for the value of property if it is lost or damaged.

manufacture The making of products by hand or machinery.

raw Something that is not processed and is still in its original state.

research Careful study and investigation for the purpose of discovering and explaining new knowledge or to collect information.

review To discuss the quality of something.

vehicle Something used to transport persons or goods.

warehouse A building for the storage of goods.

For More Information

Books

Connolly, Sean. *Getting the Message: Advertisements*. Mankato, MN: Smart Apple Media, 2010.

Larson, Jennifer S. *Who's Buying? Who's Selling? Understanding Consumers and Producers*. Minneapolis, MN: Lerner Publishing, 2010.

Mitten, Ellen. *Consumers and Producers*. Vero Beach, FL: Rourke Publishing, 2011.

Nelson, Robin. *What Do We Buy? A Look at Goods and Services*. Minneapolis, MN: Lerner Publishing, 2010.

Simons, Rae. *Spending Money*. Broomall, PA: Mason Crest, 2010.

Wittekind, Erika. *The Big Push: How Popular Culture Is Always Selling*. Mankato, MN: Compass Point Books, 2012.

Websites

Because of the changing nature of Internet links, Rosen Publishing has developed an online list of websites related to the subject of this book. This site is updated regularly. Please use this link to access the list:

http://www.rosenlinks.com/LFO/prod

INDEX